Overcoming Smoking, Alcohol, and Drug Addiction

C. P. Kumar
Reiki Healer
Roorkee - 247667, India

Disclaimer

While every effort has been made to ensure the accuracy and completeness of the content in this book, the author cannot guarantee that the information contained herein is error-free, up-to-date, or suitable for every individual circumstance.

The author shall not be held liable or responsible for any errors or omissions in the content of the book, nor for any damages, or losses that may arise from any actions taken based upon the suggestions or contents presented in the book.

Readers are advised to use their own judgment and discretion in applying the information provided in this book, and to consult with qualified professionals before taking any action based on the contents of this book. The author disclaims any and all liability or responsibility for any actions taken or not taken based on the information contained in this book.

DEDICATION

To all those who have battled their inner demons,
To those who have faced the depths of addiction,
To the warriors who have fought tirelessly for their freedom,
This book is dedicated to you.

May the pages within these chapters serve as a guiding light,
A beacon of understanding, empathy, and insight,
As you journey through the tumultuous sea of addiction,
Remember that you are never alone, and hope is your conviction.

To the individuals who dare to break the chains that bind,
Who strive for a life of clarity, purpose, and peace of mind,
Your strength is an inspiration, your courage a flame,
May this book offer tools for your victory in this noble game.

With gratitude to the countless souls who shared their stories,
Their triumphs, setbacks, and paths to glories,
Your experiences illuminate the path to recovery,
A reminder that healing is a journey of self-discovery.

As we navigate the intricacies of addiction's grasp,
May this book stand as a testament to resilience unsurpassed,
To brighter days ahead, to second chances anew,
This dedication is for you, for the battles you continue to pursue.

C. P. Kumar

CONTENTS

PREFACE

In a world where temptation lurks at every corner, where the allure of pleasure often collides with the shackles of dependence, the journey to liberation from addiction is nothing short of heroic. This book, "Overcoming Smoking, Alcohol, and Drug Addiction," stands as a guiding light in the abyss of addiction, offering a comprehensive map to reclaiming lives and rebuilding futures.

Addiction is a silent adversary that transcends borders, cultures, and backgrounds. It cunningly entwines its threads within the fabric of individual lives and societal norms, leaving in its wake a trail of broken dreams, shattered families, and untold suffering. This book is a testament to the strength of the human spirit - a resource designed to empower those ensnared by the clutches of addiction, as well as their loved ones who stand as unwavering pillars of support.

The journey commences with an exploration into the very essence of addiction. From the intricacies of neurological pathways to the psychological labyrinths that trap the mind, the book delves deep into the science behind addiction, shedding light on the darkness that often shrouds this misunderstood phenomenon.

Through meticulous research and empathetic insight, the subsequent chapters unravel the distinct threads of smoking, alcohol, and drug addiction. The pages within offer a candid glimpse into the clutches of nicotine, the deceptive allure of alcohol, and the treacherous realm of various drugs - a thorough dissection of their effects on the body, mind, and soul.

Yet, this book is not a mere exposé of addiction's grip; it is a beacon of hope for those seeking a way out. Genetic predispositions and environmental factors are explored, casting a light of understanding on the intricate dance between biology and circumstance that shapes vulnerability to addiction.

The interconnected web of psychological factors and the profound impact of addiction on mental health are laid bare, affirming the necessity of a holistic approach to recovery. The toll that addiction takes on physical well-being and mental equilibrium is chronicled with unflinching honesty, providing the stark reality check needed to fuel the resolve for change.

In the pursuit of redemption, this book opens the door to an array of treatment approaches. From therapeutic interventions to medication-based solutions, from rehabilitation programs to the myriad paths of recovery, the possibilities are illuminated like stars in a night sky, offering a sense of direction to those who may feel lost.

The book is not just an instructional manual. With chapters dedicated to each facet of addiction, this book endeavors to provide not just knowledge, but solace, camaraderie, and inspiration.

As the pages turn, the narrative shifts towards practicality. The strategies for quitting smoking, the stages of recovery from alcoholism, and the tools to manage drug addiction are all shared with the intent to empower change. Support for families is interwoven throughout, recognizing that the fight against addiction is a collective endeavor that requires compassion, patience, and understanding.

And so, the book culminates in a compendium of resources - a lifeline for those embarking on the road to recovery. Hotlines, organizations, online communities - these are the touchpoints that can provide the encouragement needed when the journey seems arduous.

Dear reader, within these pages, you hold the promise of transformation. Addiction's grip might be formidable, but the strength of the human spirit is unyielding. As you traverse the chapters of this book, may you find the knowledge to understand, the inspiration to overcome, and the unwavering belief that liberation from addiction is not just a distant dream, but a tangible reality within your grasp.

Your journey to overcoming addiction starts here.

C. P. Kumar
Reiki Healer
Former Scientist 'G', National Institute of Hydrology
Roorkee - 247667, India
E-mail: cpkumar@yahoo.com
Web: https://www.angelfire.com/nh/cpkumar/virgo.html

Introduction

In the realm of human behavior and psychology, addiction stands as a complex and pervasive phenomenon that has profound implications for individuals and society at large. As we delve into the topic of overcoming smoking, alcohol, and drug addiction, it is imperative to first grasp the fundamental concepts surrounding addiction itself. This chapter serves as an introduction to addiction, delving into its definition, underlying mechanisms, and the far-reaching consequences it exerts on both individuals and society.

Defining Addiction: Unraveling the Concept

1. The Nature of Addiction

Addiction, in its essence, refers to a compulsive and often uncontrollable engagement with a substance or behavior despite negative consequences. It is characterized by an overpowering desire, craving, or need that compels an individual to seek out and partake in a specific activity or consume a particular substance. The critical aspect of addiction lies in the loss of control, where the individual's rational decision-making abilities are overridden by the intense urge to engage in the addictive behavior.

2. Components of Addiction

Addiction is commonly composed of three interconnected components.

Craving: Craving is the intense desire or longing for the substance or behavior that a person is addicted to. This powerful urge can overshadow other thoughts and motivations, leading to a focused pursuit of the addictive element.

Loss of Control: One of the defining features of addiction is the inability to regulate or control the consumption of the substance or engagement in the behavior. This loss of control can manifest as unsuccessful attempts to cut down or quit despite adverse consequences.

Negative Consequences: Addiction often brings about negative physical, psychological, social, and economic consequences. These repercussions might include deteriorating health, strained relationships, financial instability, and a decline in overall well-being.

The Underlying Mechanisms of Addiction

1. Neurobiological Basis

At the core of addiction lies a complex interplay of neurobiological factors. The brain's reward system, which involves the release of neurotransmitters like dopamine, plays a pivotal role. Initially, engaging with the addictive substance or behavior triggers a surge in dopamine, leading to feelings of pleasure and reinforcement. Over time, the brain adapts to these elevated dopamine levels by reducing its sensitivity to the neurotransmitter, ultimately requiring more of the substance or behavior to achieve the same pleasurable effect. This phenomenon, known as tolerance, fuels the cycle of addiction.

2. Psychological Factors

Psychological factors also contribute significantly to the development and perpetuation of addiction. Individuals struggling with stress, anxiety, depression, or trauma may find solace in addictive substances or behaviors as a coping mechanism. The addictive element temporarily alleviates emotional distress, reinforcing its repeated use. This emotional attachment can deepen the roots of addiction, making it challenging to break free.

3. Social and Environmental Influences

The society and environment in which an individual resides also play a pivotal role in addiction. Social factors such as peer pressure, cultural norms, and the accessibility of addictive substances can influence an individual's likelihood of falling into addictive patterns. Additionally, environments laden with stressors and triggers may make it harder for individuals to resist the allure of addiction.

The Impact of Addiction on Individuals

1. Physical Health Consequences

Addiction wreaks havoc on an individual's physical health. Substance abuse, whether through smoking, alcohol, or drugs, can lead to a myriad of health issues, including lung diseases, liver damage, cardiovascular problems, and an increased risk of cancer. The toll on physical well-being is substantial and can ultimately result in a decreased quality of life and premature mortality.

2. Psychological and Emotional Toll

The psychological impact of addiction is equally devastating. Addiction often leads to a cycle of shame, guilt, and self-blame, as individuals grapple with their inability to overcome their compulsions. Moreover, the hijacking of the brain's reward system can lead to diminished feelings of pleasure from other activities, potentially contributing to conditions like depression and anxiety.

3. Strained Relationships

Addiction tends to strain relationships with family, friends, and romantic partners. The preoccupation with the addictive substance or behavior can lead to neglect of personal relationships, communication breakdowns, and conflicts. Loved ones may feel helpless, frustrated, and betrayed, further isolating the individual struggling with addiction.

4. Socioeconomic Challenges

Individuals grappling with addiction often face significant socioeconomic challenges. The costs associated with sustaining an addiction, be it financial or in terms of lost opportunities, can lead to financial instability and hinder personal and professional growth. Unemployment, legal issues, and compromised career prospects are not uncommon outcomes.

The Societal Ramifications of Addiction

1. Economic Burden

Beyond the individual level, addiction poses substantial economic burdens on society. Healthcare expenditures rise as a result of treating addiction-related health issues. Additionally, decreased workforce productivity, absenteeism, and disability claims contribute to economic losses. Governments must allocate resources to address addiction-related challenges, diverting funds from other critical areas.

2. Crime and Criminal Justice System

Addiction can drive criminal behavior as individuals seek ways to sustain their habits. This places a strain on the criminal justice system, with a significant portion of incarcerations being linked to addiction-related offenses. The cycle of addiction and crime perpetuates, creating a cycle that is hard to break without comprehensive intervention.

3. Strain on Healthcare Systems

Healthcare systems bear the brunt of addiction-related consequences. Emergency rooms and rehabilitation facilities become inundated with cases of overdose, substance-related injuries, and mental health crises. The demand for addiction treatment often exceeds the available resources, leading to gaps in care and long waitlists for those seeking help.

4. Erosion of Social Fabric

Addiction can erode the social fabric of communities. The breakdown of families, weakened social ties, and heightened stigmatization of individuals struggling with addiction can lead to fragmented communities. The lack of support and understanding exacerbates the challenges faced by those seeking recovery.

Conclusion

Addiction is a multifaceted phenomenon with far-reaching implications for individuals and society. Its definition extends beyond mere substance use to encompass the loss of control, intense craving, and negative consequences that ensue. The interplay of neurobiological, psychological, and social factors contributes to the development and persistence of addiction. Individuals grappling with addiction experience profound physical, psychological, and relational challenges, while society bears the weight of economic, criminal justice, healthcare, and social burdens.

As we embark on the journey to overcome smoking, alcohol, and drug addiction, it is crucial to understand the depth of addiction's impact. Only with a comprehensive understanding of the underlying mechanisms and societal repercussions can effective strategies be developed to break the cycle of addiction and pave the way for recovery and healing. This book seeks to provide guidance, support, and evidence-based approaches to empower individuals in their quest to overcome addiction and reclaim their lives.

Introduction

Addiction is a complex and multifaceted phenomenon that has been a subject of scientific inquiry for decades. Whether it's smoking, alcohol, drugs, or any other addictive behavior, the grip of addiction can have devastating effects on individuals and their families. To truly address and overcome addiction, it is crucial to understand the underlying neurological and psychological mechanisms that drive these behaviors. This chapter delves into the science of addiction, shedding light on the intricate interplay between the brain, behavior, and environment.

Neurological Underpinnings of Addiction

1. The Reward Pathway and Dopamine

At the core of addiction lies the brain's reward pathway, a network of interconnected structures that govern our experiences of pleasure and reinforcement. Dopamine, a neurotransmitter, plays a pivotal role in this process. When we engage in pleasurable activities, such as eating, socializing, or using substances, the brain releases dopamine, leading to a sense of enjoyment and motivation to repeat the behavior.

2. The Role of the Mesolimbic Pathway

The mesolimbic pathway, often referred to as the brain's "reward circuit," is a critical component of the reward system. This pathway connects the ventral tegmental area (VTA), a region deep in the brain, to the nucleus accumbens and other areas involved in motivation and emotion. The release of dopamine in response to rewarding stimuli strengthens the neural connections associated with the behavior, reinforcing the desire to engage in it again.

3. Neuroplasticity and Conditioning

Repeated exposure to addictive substances or behaviors can lead to changes in the brain's structure and function. Neuroplasticity, the brain's ability to reorganize itself in response to experiences, plays a role in addiction. Through a process known as conditioning, the brain associates cues and environments with the rewarding effects of addictive substances. Over time, these cues can trigger cravings and anticipation of pleasure, making it challenging to break the cycle of addiction.

The Role of Genetics

Genetic Vulnerability

Genetics also contribute significantly to addiction susceptibility. Certain individuals may possess genetic variations that predispose them to addictive behaviors. For example, variations in genes related to dopamine receptors or the body's ability to metabolize substances can influence an individual's response to addictive substances. While genetics can increase the risk of addiction, they do not determine it outright. Environmental factors and personal choices play a crucial role in whether an individual develops an addiction.

Psychological Factors in Addiction

1. Co-Occurring Mental Health Disorders

Addiction is often intertwined with mental health disorders such as depression, anxiety, or trauma. Individuals may turn to addictive substances or behaviors as a way to self-medicate or alleviate emotional distress. The relationship between addiction and mental health is bidirectional, with one condition exacerbating the other. Integrated treatment approaches that address both addiction and mental health are essential for effective recovery.

2. Stress and Coping Mechanisms

Stress is a significant trigger for addictive behaviors. Chronic stress can dysregulate the brain's reward system and increase susceptibility to addiction. People may turn to substances or behaviors as a way to cope with stress, as these activities provide temporary relief. Over time, the brain associates the addictive behavior with stress relief, making it challenging to break the cycle. Developing healthy coping mechanisms and stress management strategies is a crucial aspect of overcoming addiction.

3. Conditioning and Environmental Cues

Environmental cues play a pivotal role in addiction maintenance. Just as the brain forms associations between cues and rewards, it also establishes connections between cues and cravings. These cues can be as subtle as a specific smell, location, or time of day. Exposure to these cues can trigger powerful cravings and automatic responses that drive addictive behaviors. Recognizing and managing these cues is vital for preventing relapse.

The Role of Reinforcement Learning

1. Reinforcement Learning Model

A psychological perspective on addiction involves the concept of reinforcement learning. This model explains how individuals learn to choose behaviors that maximize rewards and minimize negative outcomes. In the context of addiction, substance use initially provides intense rewards, which reinforces the behavior. However, as tolerance develops, individuals require more of the substance to achieve the same reward, leading to a cycle of escalation and addiction.

2. Delay Discounting and Impulsivity

Addiction often involves a struggle between immediate gratification and long-term consequences. Delay discounting refers to the tendency to value immediate rewards more than future rewards. Individuals with addiction tend to exhibit higher levels of impulsivity and are more likely to choose immediate rewards, even when they are aware of the negative consequences. Understanding the role of impulsivity can inform interventions that promote better decision-making in the face of addiction triggers.

Neurobiology of Withdrawal and Cravings

1. Hedonic Dysregulation

With prolonged substance use, the brain's reward system can become dysregulated. This phenomenon, known as hedonic dysregulation, leads to a reduced ability to experience pleasure from natural rewards. As a result, individuals become increasingly reliant on the addictive substance to achieve a sense of pleasure and normalcy. Withdrawal symptoms, which occur when the substance is not present, can intensify cravings and reinforce the cycle of addiction.

2. Altered Stress Responses

Chronic substance use can also impact the brain's stress response system. Over time, the brain becomes sensitized to stress, leading to heightened stress responses. This sensitization can lead to a negative cycle where stress triggers cravings, and substance use provides temporary stress relief. The gradual erosion of the brain's ability to regulate stress contributes to the persistence of addiction.

The Road to Recovery

1. Neuroplasticity and Rehabilitation

While addiction changes the brain, it is important to recognize that the brain remains adaptable throughout life. This concept of neuroplasticity means that the brain can rewire itself in response to new experiences and behaviors. Rehabilitation and recovery involve rewiring the brain to associate rewards with healthier behaviors. This process requires time, effort, and the development of new habits and coping strategies.

2. Therapeutic Interventions

A variety of therapeutic approaches have been developed to address addiction from both neurological and psychological perspectives. Behavioral therapies, such as cognitive-behavioral therapy (CBT) and contingency management, help individuals recognize and modify the thoughts and behaviors that contribute to addiction. Pharmacological interventions, when appropriate, can also aid in managing withdrawal symptoms and reducing cravings.

The environment plays a crucial role in addiction recovery. Support systems, including family, friends, and support groups, provide the social and emotional scaffolding necessary for individuals to navigate the challenges of recovery. Creating an environment that minimizes exposure to addictive cues and maximizes opportunities for positive reinforcement is essential for long-term success.

Conclusion

Understanding the science of addiction is a critical step toward overcoming its grip. Neurological and psychological mechanisms intersect to create a complex web of behaviors and responses. By addressing the reward system, genetics, psychological factors, and the role of learning, we can develop comprehensive strategies to combat addiction. Recovery is a journey that requires rewiring the brain, reshaping behaviors, and rebuilding support networks. Armed with scientific knowledge and a multidimensional approach, individuals can pave the way toward a life free from the chains of addiction.

Introduction

In the realm of addictive substances, nicotine holds a notorious position as one of the most addictive chemicals known to humanity. Smoking, primarily driven by nicotine addiction, is a global health concern that affects millions of lives. This chapter aims to delve into the addictive nature of nicotine and shed light on the challenges individuals face when attempting to quit smoking. By understanding the physiological and psychological mechanisms behind nicotine addiction, as well as the obstacles encountered during the quitting process, we can provide valuable insights into effective strategies for overcoming smoking addiction.

Nicotine: The Addictive Culprit

Nicotine, a naturally occurring compound found in tobacco leaves, is the driving force behind the addictive nature of smoking. Its rapid absorption into the bloodstream and brain leads to an almost instantaneous release of dopamine, a neurotransmitter associated with pleasure and reward. This dopamine surge creates a reinforcing loop that strengthens the desire to continue smoking.

1. Dopamine and Reward Pathways

Nicotine hijacks the brain's reward pathways, creating an artificial sense of pleasure and euphoria. The release of dopamine reinforces the association between smoking and feeling good, leading to a powerful psychological attachment to the habit. Over time, this association becomes deeply ingrained, making it challenging for individuals to break free from the cycle of smoking.

2. Neuroadaptation and Tolerance

With prolonged nicotine exposure, the brain undergoes neuroadaptation to counteract the constant dopamine overload. This results in a phenomenon known as tolerance, where individuals require higher doses of nicotine to achieve the same pleasurable effects. Tolerance further fuels the addictive cycle, as smokers often increase their consumption to maintain the desired sensations, leading to greater physiological dependence.

Psychological and Behavioral Aspects of Smoking Addiction

Beyond its physiological effects, smoking addiction is deeply intertwined with psychological and behavioral factors. Understanding these aspects is crucial for developing comprehensive strategies to overcome addiction.

1. Habitual Associations

Smoking becomes intertwined with various daily activities and emotions, forming habitual associations. Whether it's smoking after meals, during breaks, or in times of stress, these associations contribute to the difficulty of quitting. Breaking these habits requires addressing the psychological triggers that prompt the urge to smoke.

2. Coping Mechanism

For many individuals, smoking serves as a coping mechanism to deal with stress, anxiety, and negative emotions. The ritual of lighting a cigarette becomes a way to temporarily alleviate emotional discomfort. This emotional dependence complicates the quitting process, as individuals fear losing their primary coping strategy.

3. Social and Environmental Influences

Social and environmental factors play a significant role in sustaining smoking addiction. Peer pressure, exposure to smoking in social settings, and the normalization of smoking in certain cultures can all contribute to the difficulty of quitting. Overcoming these influences requires building a strong support system and developing alternative social activities.

Challenges of Quitting Smoking

Quitting smoking is a commendable but often arduous journey. The challenges faced during this process are multifaceted and require a comprehensive approach.

1. Nicotine Withdrawal

One of the most significant obstacles to quitting smoking is nicotine withdrawal. As the body adjusts to the absence of nicotine, individuals experience a range of withdrawal symptoms, including irritability, anxiety, depression, and intense cravings. These symptoms can be overwhelming and lead to relapse if not managed effectively.

2. Relapse Triggers

The journey to quit smoking is rarely linear, and relapses are common. Certain triggers, such as encountering stress, being in the presence of other smokers, or facing emotional upheavals, can lead to relapse. Acknowledging these triggers and developing coping strategies to navigate them is crucial for maintaining long-term abstinence.

3. Psychological Warfare

The psychological aspect of quitting smoking can be likened to a battle within one's mind. The inner dialogue between the desire to quit and the allure of smoking can create immense internal conflict. Individuals often grapple with feelings of self-doubt, questioning their willpower and ability to overcome the addiction.

4. Long-term Changes

Quitting smoking requires not only overcoming immediate challenges but also making long-term lifestyle changes. This includes rewiring the brain's associations with smoking, finding alternative coping mechanisms, and redefining one's identity as a non-smoker. Such changes demand dedication, patience, and a strong commitment to personal growth.

Strategies for Overcoming Smoking Addiction

While the challenges of quitting smoking are formidable, a range of strategies can empower individuals to overcome their addiction and lead healthier lives.

1. Nicotine Replacement Therapy (NRT)

NRT involves using products like nicotine gum, patches, and lozenges to gradually reduce nicotine intake while minimizing withdrawal symptoms. These products provide a controlled way to wean off nicotine and can increase the chances of successful quitting.

2. Behavioral Therapy

Behavioral therapies, such as cognitive-behavioral therapy (CBT), focus on identifying and modifying the thoughts, emotions, and behaviors associated with smoking. By addressing the psychological components of addiction, individuals can develop healthier coping strategies and break free from habitual associations.

3. Support Systems

Having a strong support system is invaluable during the quitting process. Whether through friends, family, support groups, or counseling, having individuals who understand the challenges and offer encouragement can significantly enhance one's chances of success.

4. Mindfulness and Stress Reduction

Practices like mindfulness meditation and yoga can help individuals manage stress, anxiety, and cravings. These techniques cultivate present-moment awareness and provide tools to navigate triggers without resorting to smoking.

5. Pharmacotherapy

Prescription medications, such as varenicline and bupropion, can assist in quitting by reducing nicotine cravings and withdrawal symptoms. However, these medications should be used under medical supervision due to potential side effects.

The Journey to Freedom

Overcoming smoking addiction is a journey that requires a combination of physiological, psychological, and social strategies. Understanding the addictive nature of nicotine, addressing the psychological facets of smoking, and employing effective quitting strategies are essential steps toward lasting freedom from addiction. While the path may be challenging, the rewards of improved health, increased quality of life, and renewed self-control are well worth the effort. Remember, quitting smoking is not just an end to an addiction; it's a transformational journey toward a brighter, smoke-free future.

Conclusion

Smoking addiction, fueled by nicotine's potent grasp on the brain's reward system, presents formidable challenges for those seeking to quit. The intertwined psychological, behavioral, and physiological aspects of addiction make the journey to freedom complex and demanding. However, armed with knowledge, strategies, and support, individuals can break the chains of smoking addiction and embark on a path of improved well-being and self-discovery. As we continue to explore the depths of addiction and recovery, a comprehensive understanding of nicotine's addictive nature and the obstacles of quitting smoking will contribute to the arsenal of tools we can offer to those in pursuit of a healthier, addiction-free life.

Introduction

In the journey to overcome addiction, understanding the intricate relationship between substances and their impact on the human body is crucial. Alcohol addiction is a widespread issue that affects millions of individuals globally. This chapter aims to delve into the multifaceted effects of alcohol on the brain, body, and behavior, shedding light on the complexities of alcohol addiction and offering insights into how to overcome it.

The Brain's Reward System and Dopamine

Alcohol addiction is closely linked to the brain's reward system, a complex network that reinforces behaviors necessary for survival. Central to this system is dopamine, a neurotransmitter that plays a pivotal role in feelings of pleasure and reward. When alcohol is consumed, it triggers the release of dopamine, leading to a sense of euphoria. This pleasurable sensation reinforces the desire to consume alcohol, creating a cycle that can develop into addiction.

Neuroplasticity and Adaptation

Continued alcohol consumption can lead to neuroplastic changes in the brain. The brain adapts to the presence of alcohol by reducing its sensitivity to dopamine, resulting in a diminished response to pleasurable stimuli. This phenomenon drives individuals to consume larger quantities of alcohol to achieve the same level of satisfaction, fostering a cycle of increasing consumption and tolerance.

Impact on the Central Nervous System

Alcohol's effects extend beyond the brain's reward system, affecting the central nervous system as a whole. Alcohol is a depressant that slows down neural activity, leading to various cognitive and physical effects.

1. Impaired Cognitive Functions

Chronic alcohol use can impair cognitive functions such as memory, attention, and decision-making. The hippocampus, a region crucial for memory consolidation, is particularly vulnerable to the toxic effects of alcohol. This impairment can contribute to poor judgment and impulsive behavior often seen in individuals struggling with alcohol addiction.

2. Disruption of Neurotransmitter Balance

Alcohol also interferes with the delicate balance of neurotransmitters in the brain. GABA, another neurotransmitter, is enhanced by alcohol, contributing to the sedative effects of the substance. On the other hand, glutamate, which promotes neural excitation, is suppressed. Sudden cessation of alcohol consumption can lead to a surge in glutamate, causing withdrawal symptoms and reinforcing the cycle of addiction.

Physical and Behavioral Consequences

Beyond its neurological impact, alcohol addiction wreaks havoc on the body and behavior.

The liver bears the brunt of alcohol's impact, as it is responsible for metabolizing the substance. Prolonged alcohol consumption can lead to fatty liver, alcoholic hepatitis, and cirrhosis. These conditions not only endanger physical health but also contribute to a cycle of addiction, as individuals may continue drinking despite knowing the consequences.

Alcohol addiction doesn't occur in isolation; it affects an individual's behavior and social interactions. Relationships can deteriorate due to erratic behavior, neglect of responsibilities, and impaired decision-making. Occupational and academic performance may suffer, exacerbating feelings of guilt and shame.

The Role of Genetics

Genetics play a significant role in alcohol addiction susceptibility. Certain genetic variations can influence an individual's response to alcohol, affecting their likelihood of developing an addiction.

Genetic Predisposition

Family and twin studies have revealed that alcohol use disorder (AUD) has a hereditary component. Certain genes are associated with an increased risk of developing AUD, including those involved in dopamine regulation and alcohol metabolism. However, genetics are not the sole determinant; environmental factors also play a crucial role.

Overcoming Alcohol Addiction

While alcohol addiction is a formidable challenge, recovery is possible through a comprehensive and multifaceted approach.

1. Medical Detoxification

For individuals with severe alcohol dependence, medical detoxification may be necessary. This involves supervised withdrawal, often accompanied by medication to alleviate withdrawal symptoms and reduce the risk of seizures.

2. Psychotherapy and Behavioral Interventions

Therapies such as cognitive-behavioral therapy (CBT) and motivational enhancement therapy (MET) can help individuals identify triggers, develop coping mechanisms, and modify behaviors associated with alcohol consumption. Support groups like Alcoholics Anonymous (AA) https://www.aa.org/ provide a platform for sharing experiences and fostering a sense of community.

3. Addressing Underlying Mental Health Issues

Many individuals with alcohol addiction have co-occurring mental health disorders such as depression, anxiety, or trauma. Treating these underlying issues is crucial for sustained recovery, often requiring a combination of therapy and medication.

4. Holistic Approaches

Holistic approaches, including mindfulness, meditation, and yoga, can complement traditional therapies by promoting self-awareness, emotional regulation, and stress reduction.

5. Rebuilding a Supportive Environment

Recovery is significantly aided by a supportive environment. Family, friends, and healthcare professionals can provide invaluable encouragement and accountability throughout the journey.

Conclusion

Alcohol addiction's impact on the brain, body, and behavior underscores the complexity of the disorder. Understanding the mechanisms by which alcohol affects the brain's reward system, disrupts neurotransmitter balance, and influences behavior is vital for effective treatment and recovery. Overcoming alcohol addiction requires a comprehensive approach that addresses the physical, psychological, and social aspects of the disorder. By combining medical interventions, therapy, and holistic practices within a supportive environment, individuals can embark on a path to recovery and rediscover a life free from the grips of alcohol addiction.

Introduction

In the modern world, drug addiction has become a pressing issue affecting individuals from all walks of life. The allure of various types of drugs, each with its own addictive properties, has ensnared countless lives in a cycle of dependence and despair. Understanding the different types of drugs, their addictive potentials, and the inherent dangers they pose is essential in addressing this global crisis. This chapter aims to provide a comprehensive overview of drug addiction, shedding light on the diverse substances that contribute to the problem.

Types of Drugs and Their Addictive Properties

1. Stimulants

Stimulants are a class of drugs that increase activity in the central nervous system, resulting in heightened alertness, energy, and euphoria. Substances like cocaine, amphetamines, and methamphetamines fall into this category. These drugs impact the brain's dopamine levels, creating intense pleasure and a desire for repeated use.

Stimulants are particularly addictive due to their rapid onset of effects and the intense reward they provide. Users may experience a sense of invincibility and heightened self-esteem, making it challenging to resist repeated use. Over time, the brain becomes dependent on the increased dopamine release caused by stimulants, leading to cravings and addiction.

2. Depressants

Depressant drugs, in contrast, slow down the central nervous system's activity, inducing relaxation and sedation. This category includes substances like alcohol, benzodiazepines, and certain sleep medications. Depressants have a calming effect on the brain, often used to alleviate anxiety and stress.

The addictive nature of depressants stems from their ability to induce a sense of relief and relaxation. Individuals with anxiety or insomnia may find these substances temporarily comforting, leading to misuse and dependence. Prolonged use can lead to tolerance, necessitating higher doses to achieve the desired effect, which increases the risk of addiction.

3. Opioids

Opioids are powerful pain-relieving drugs that also produce feelings of euphoria and relaxation. Prescription painkillers like oxycodone and illicit substances like heroin belong to this category. Opioids bind to specific receptors in the brain, spinal cord, and gastrointestinal tract, reducing the perception of pain and inducing pleasure.

The danger of opioid addiction lies in the ease with which physical dependence develops. Prolonged use can lead to the body's tolerance and withdrawal symptoms when not using the drug. This cycle of pain relief, euphoria, and withdrawal makes breaking free from opioid addiction exceptionally challenging.

4. Hallucinogens

Hallucinogenic drugs alter perception, thoughts, and feelings, often leading to vivid hallucinations. Substances like LSD, psilocybin (magic mushrooms), and MDMA (ecstasy) fall into this category. Hallucinogens affect the brain's serotonin receptors, causing changes in mood and sensory experiences.

While not as inherently addictive as stimulants or opioids, hallucinogens can still lead to problematic use. The allure of altered perceptions and spiritual experiences can lead to repeated use, especially in social or party settings. However, the unpredictable nature of hallucinogens and the potential for adverse psychological reactions can deter consistent use for many individuals.

Dangers Posed by Drug Addiction

1. Physical Health Risks

Drug addiction takes a toll on the body's physical health, leading to a range of serious medical issues. For instance, stimulant use can result in heart problems, such as irregular heartbeats and high blood pressure. Opioid abuse increases the risk of respiratory depression and overdose. Liver damage and neurological issues are common among those who misuse depressants like alcohol.

2. Mental Health Implications

The link between drug addiction and mental health cannot be overstated. Prolonged drug use can lead to or exacerbate mental health disorders like anxiety, depression, and schizophrenia. The cycle of addiction often worsens these conditions, creating a downward spiral where individuals use drugs to self-medicate, only to find their mental health deteriorating further.

Drug addiction reverberates beyond the individual, impacting their relationships, work, and overall social integration. Strained relationships with family and friends are common, as the pursuit of drugs often takes precedence over personal connections. Job loss, financial instability, and legal troubles frequently follow addiction, perpetuating a cycle of despair.

One of the gravest dangers of drug addiction is the risk of overdose and death. As individuals build tolerance, they require higher doses to achieve the same effects, increasing the chances of accidental overdose. Opioids, in particular, have been responsible for a significant portion of overdose-related deaths, devastating families and communities.

The long-term consequences of drug addiction are far-reaching. Chronic health issues, damaged relationships, legal entanglements, and financial ruin are often the legacy of addiction. Even after achieving sobriety, individuals may struggle with cravings and the psychological impact of their past behavior, making relapse a constant threat.

Conclusion

In the battle against drug addiction, knowledge is the most potent weapon. Understanding the various types of drugs, their addictive properties, and the dangers they pose is crucial for both prevention and treatment. By shedding light on the physical, mental, and social implications of drug addiction, we pave the way for a more informed and compassionate approach to helping individuals break free from the clutches of substance abuse. This chapter has provided a glimpse into the complex world of drug addiction, emphasizing the urgency of addressing this issue as we strive to create a healthier, addiction-free society.

Introduction

Addiction, whether to substances like smoking, alcohol, or drugs, is a complex phenomenon that arises from a combination of various factors. Among these factors, genetics plays a significant role in determining an individual's susceptibility to addiction. The interplay between genetic predisposition and environmental influences can profoundly impact an individual's likelihood of developing addictive behaviors. This chapter delves into the intricate relationship between genetics and addiction, exploring how genetic factors contribute to susceptibility and what this means for individuals seeking to overcome addiction.

Understanding Genetic Predisposition

1. The Role of Genes

Genes are the fundamental units of heredity, carrying instructions for building and maintaining the body's structures and functions. They also influence an individual's vulnerability to various health conditions, including addiction. Genetic predisposition refers to the increased likelihood of an individual developing a particular condition due to the presence of specific genes. In the context of addiction, certain genetic variants can contribute to an enhanced susceptibility to addictive substances.

2. Complex Inheritance Patterns

The inheritance of addiction susceptibility is not governed by a single gene, but rather by a complex interplay of multiple genes. Polygenic inheritance, where many genes contribute to a trait, is observed in addiction susceptibility. This complexity makes it challenging to pinpoint specific genes responsible for addiction, as well as to predict an individual's risk solely based on their genetic makeup.

Genetic Factors in Addiction Susceptibility

1. Dopamine Receptors and Reward Pathways

One of the key players in addiction susceptibility is the dopamine system, particularly dopamine receptors in the brain's reward pathways. Dopamine is a neurotransmitter associated with pleasure and reward. Genetic variations in dopamine receptor genes can influence an individual's response to pleasurable stimuli, impacting their susceptibility to addiction. For example, variations in the DRD2 gene have been linked to differences in dopamine receptor density, affecting how individuals experience rewards and potentially driving addictive behaviors.

2. Metabolism of Substances

Genetic variations can also affect how the body metabolizes addictive substances. Enzymes responsible for breaking down these substances can differ among individuals due to genetic factors. For instance, variations in the genes encoding alcohol-metabolizing enzymes like alcohol dehydrogenase (ADH) and aldehyde dehydrogenase (ALDH) can influence an individual's tolerance to alcohol. Slow metabolizers may experience unpleasant side effects such as flushing and nausea, leading to a reduced likelihood of excessive drinking, while fast metabolizers might be more prone to heavy drinking and alcohol dependence.

3. Impulse Control and Decision-Making

Certain genetic variants are associated with altered impulse control and decision-making processes. The COMT gene, for instance, influences dopamine breakdown in the brain and has been linked to impulsive behavior. Individuals with specific variants of this gene may have difficulty regulating their impulses, making them more susceptible to addiction. Impaired decision-making, often seen in addiction, can also be influenced by genetic factors, such as variations in the BDNF gene, which is involved in synaptic plasticity and cognitive function.

Gene-Environment Interaction

1. The Influence of Environmental Factors

While genetic predisposition is a crucial factor in addiction susceptibility, it does not act in isolation. Environmental factors play a significant role in shaping whether genetic predispositions manifest as addictive behaviors. Stress, trauma, peer influence, socioeconomic status, and availability of addictive substances are among the environmental factors that can trigger or suppress addictive tendencies.

2. Epigenetics: Bridging the Gap

Epigenetics, the study of changes in gene expression without altering the underlying DNA sequence, provides insights into how genetic and environmental factors interact. Epigenetic modifications can be influenced by experiences and exposures, effectively "turning on" or "turning off" specific genes. This interplay can either enhance or mitigate an individual's genetic predisposition to addiction. Epigenetic changes resulting from environmental factors can persist across generations, further shaping susceptibility to addiction.

Genetic Testing and Addiction Risk

1. The Promise of Genetic Testing

Advancements in genetic research have led to the development of genetic tests aimed at assessing an individual's susceptibility to addiction. These tests analyze specific genetic markers associated with addiction vulnerability. While these tests can offer valuable insights, their predictive accuracy is limited due to the multifaceted nature of addiction susceptibility.

2. Ethical Considerations

The use of genetic testing for addiction susceptibility raises ethical concerns. Privacy, informed consent, and potential psychological impacts must be carefully considered. A positive result from such a test could lead to unnecessary distress, while a negative result might falsely reassure individuals about their risk, potentially encouraging risky behaviors.

Implications for Overcoming Addiction

1. A Holistic Approach

Understanding the role of genetics in addiction susceptibility underscores the importance of a holistic approach to overcoming addiction. Recognizing that genetics is just one piece of the puzzle, individuals struggling with addiction can benefit from comprehensive interventions that address both genetic predisposition and environmental influences.

2. Personalized Treatment Plans

Genetic information can guide the development of personalized treatment plans. By identifying genetic markers associated with addiction susceptibility, healthcare providers can tailor interventions to address an individual's unique needs. This might involve utilizing medications that target specific genetic factors or designing behavioral therapies that align with an individual's genetic predisposition.

3. Environmental Modifications

Recognizing the influence of environmental factors, individuals seeking to overcome addiction can make conscious efforts to modify their surroundings. This might involve distancing themselves from triggering environments or seeking supportive social networks that facilitate recovery. Understanding one's genetic predisposition can empower individuals to proactively shape their environment in ways that mitigate their vulnerability to addiction.

Conclusion

Genetic predisposition plays a significant role in an individual's susceptibility to addiction, interacting intricately with environmental factors. The complex interplay between genetics and addiction underscores the need for personalized approaches to treatment and recovery. While genetic testing holds promise, ethical considerations and the multifactorial nature of addiction susceptibility remind us that genetics is only one aspect of the larger picture. By embracing a holistic perspective and leveraging our understanding of genetics, individuals can better navigate the challenges of overcoming smoking, alcohol, and drug addiction.

Introduction

Addiction is a complex and multifaceted issue that affects individuals across the globe, spanning a wide range of substances including smoking, alcohol, and drugs. While genetic and biological factors certainly play a role in addiction development, it's becoming increasingly evident that environmental influences also play a significant part. This chapter delves into the intricate relationship between environmental factors, upbringing, and peer influence in the context of addiction development, offering insights into how understanding these elements can contribute to overcoming addiction.

The Interplay of Nature and Nurture

1. Genetic Predisposition

Genetic factors can lay the foundation for addiction vulnerability. Certain individuals may possess genetic variations that affect their response to substances, influencing the likelihood of addiction development. However, genetics alone cannot predict addiction; environmental factors play a pivotal role in determining whether these genetic predispositions will manifest.

2. The Environmental Trigger

While genetics may set the stage, environmental factors often serve as the catalysts that lead to addiction. Exposure to substances, particularly during critical developmental periods, can significantly impact an individual's susceptibility to addiction. The environment in which one grows up, their upbringing, and the people they interact with all contribute to shaping their attitudes and behaviors toward substances.

The Role of Upbringing

1. Family Dynamics

The family unit is a cornerstone of upbringing, and its dynamics can profoundly influence addiction development. Children raised in households where substance use is normalized or witnessed are more likely to view these behaviors as acceptable. Parental substance abuse can expose children to these habits at an early age, potentially normalizing the behavior and increasing the likelihood of experimentation and later addiction.

2. Parental Modeling

Parents serve as role models for their children, and their behaviors, attitudes, and communication styles significantly impact the child's perceptions of substances. Children who observe responsible substance use or conversations that emphasize the risks and consequences of addiction are more likely to adopt a cautious and informed approach toward substances. On the other hand, children exposed to parental substance abuse are at higher risk of mirroring these behaviors.

3. Emotional Environment

The emotional climate at home plays a pivotal role in addiction susceptibility. Children raised in environments characterized by neglect, abuse, or emotional instability may turn to substances as a coping mechanism. The lack of healthy coping strategies can lead to seeking solace in substances, ultimately paving the way for addiction.

Peer Influence: The Power of Social Circles

1. The Impact of Peer Pressure

During adolescence, peers become increasingly influential. The desire to fit in and be accepted can override an individual's better judgment, leading to experimentation with substances. Peer pressure can be subtle or overt, pushing individuals to engage in behaviors they might not otherwise consider.

2. Identity and Belonging

Belonging to a peer group that condones or promotes substance use can become a crucial aspect of an individual's identity. The need to maintain that identity and uphold group norms can lead to continued substance use, eventually resulting in addiction. Conversely, peer groups that discourage substance use and promote healthy behaviors can act as protective factors.

3. Online and Virtual Peer Influence

In today's digital age, peer influence extends beyond physical interactions. Online communities and social media platforms provide spaces where individuals can connect with others who share similar substance-related interests. These virtual networks can either amplify positive messages of recovery or normalize addictive behaviors, depending on the content and interactions within these online spaces.

Socioeconomic Factors

1. Economic Disparities

Socioeconomic status can significantly impact addiction development. Individuals facing economic hardships may turn to substances as a means of escape or coping with stressors. Limited access to quality education, healthcare, and social support systems can exacerbate the challenges of addiction recovery for those in lower socioeconomic strata.

2. Availability and Accessibility

The availability and accessibility of substances also play a critical role. Areas with high concentrations of liquor stores or easy access to drugs can increase the likelihood of experimentation and habitual use. Regulatory measures that limit substance availability can act as a deterrent and reduce the prevalence of addiction.

Environmental Interventions and Support

1. Preventive Measures

Understanding the intricate interplay between environment, upbringing, and peer influence allows for the implementation of targeted preventive measures. Educational campaigns that raise awareness about the risks of addiction, especially during adolescence, can equip individuals with the knowledge to make informed decisions. Schools, parents, and communities can collaborate to provide comprehensive substance education.

2. Family-Centered Approaches

Incorporating family-centered approaches into addiction prevention and treatment can yield significant results. Offering support and education to parents can help them create nurturing environments that discourage substance use. Family therapy and counseling can address underlying family dynamics that contribute to addictive behaviors.

3. Community Support Systems

Communities play a vital role in shaping individuals' environments. Establishing support systems that promote healthy activities and discourage substance use can create an environment conducive to recovery. Community centers, mentorship programs, and recreational facilities can offer alternatives to substance-related activities.

4. Peer-Led Interventions

Harnessing the power of positive peer influence, peer-led interventions can be effective in preventing and overcoming addiction. Peers who have successfully overcome addiction can serve as role models and provide support to those currently struggling. Peer support groups and mentoring programs create spaces where individuals can connect with others who understand their challenges.

Conclusion

The journey from experimentation to addiction is influenced by a complex interplay of environmental factors, upbringing, and peer influence. Genetics may set the stage, but it is the environment that often triggers and perpetuates addictive behaviors. Recognizing the significance of these factors opens the door to targeted interventions and support systems that can prevent addiction and aid in recovery. By addressing family dynamics, promoting healthy peer interactions, and creating supportive communities, we can collectively work towards overcoming the grasp of addiction and building a healthier future.

Introduction

In the battle against addiction, it is essential to recognize the intricate interplay between mental health disorders and addictive behaviors. The relationship between these two factors is a complex and multidimensional one, often leading to a vicious cycle that can be challenging to break free from. This chapter delves into the psychological factors that underpin the connection between mental health disorders and addiction, shedding light on the mechanisms at play and exploring strategies for overcoming these intertwined challenges.

The Bidirectional Relationship: Mental Health Disorders and Addiction

1. Shared Vulnerabilities

Mental health disorders and addiction share a common ground when it comes to vulnerabilities. Research has shown that individuals who suffer from conditions like anxiety, depression, and post-traumatic stress disorder (PTSD) are more likely to turn to addictive substances or behaviors as a coping mechanism. The intense emotional distress that accompanies these disorders can lead individuals to seek relief through substances like nicotine, alcohol, or drugs.

2. Self-Medication Hypothesis

The self-medication hypothesis offers insights into why individuals with mental health disorders might be more prone to addiction. According to this theory, people may use substances as a way to alleviate the distressing symptoms of their mental health conditions. For instance, someone grappling with social anxiety might rely on alcohol to ease their inhibitions in social situations. While this may provide temporary relief, it often exacerbates the underlying mental health disorder and contributes to the development of addiction.

Neurobiological Connections

1. The Role of Reward Pathways

Both addiction and mental health disorders are associated with disruptions in the brain's reward pathways. The mesolimbic dopamine system, often referred to as the brain's "pleasure center," plays a crucial role in reinforcing behaviors that are pleasurable or rewarding. In individuals with mental health disorders, this system may be dysregulated, leading to a reduced capacity to experience pleasure from natural rewards. This can increase susceptibility to addictive substances or behaviors, as they can artificially stimulate the brain's reward system.

2. Common Neurotransmitters

Serotonin, dopamine, and norepinephrine are neurotransmitters that have been implicated in both mental health disorders and addiction. Imbalances in these neurotransmitter systems are associated with conditions like depression, anxiety, and attention-deficit hyperactivity disorder (ADHD). Interestingly, these imbalances can also make individuals more susceptible to addictive behaviors. For instance, nicotine can enhance dopamine release, offering a temporary mood boost for those dealing with depressive symptoms.

The Role of Trauma

1. Complex Trauma and Coping Mechanisms

Experiences of trauma, whether in the form of physical abuse, sexual assault, or emotional neglect, can significantly impact mental health. Individuals who have undergone trauma often develop coping mechanisms to deal with the overwhelming emotions that arise. Unfortunately, some of these coping strategies may involve turning to addictive substances or behaviors as a way to numb emotional pain or regain a sense of control.

2. Trauma's Impact on Self-Worth

Trauma can deeply affect an individual's sense of self-worth and identity. This can create a fertile ground for addiction, as substances or behaviors that provide temporary relief from feelings of shame, guilt, or inadequacy are more likely to be sought out. Over time, the repeated use of these substances can lead to a cycle of dependence that further erodes self-esteem, perpetuating the addiction.

Breaking the Cycle: Strategies for Overcoming Dual Diagnosis

1. Integrated Treatment Approaches

Addressing both the mental health disorder and the addiction concurrently is crucial for successful recovery. Integrated treatment approaches that combine psychotherapy, medication, and behavioral interventions have shown promising results. Therapies like Cognitive Behavioral Therapy (CBT) can help individuals recognize and change negative thought patterns, reducing the need for self-medication through addictive substances.

2. Support Networks and Peer Groups

Building a strong support network is invaluable for individuals navigating the complex terrain of mental health disorders and addiction. Peer support groups provide a safe space to share experiences, offer encouragement, and learn coping strategies from others who have faced similar challenges. Connecting with individuals who understand the unique struggles of dual diagnosis can foster a sense of belonging and reduce feelings of isolation.

3. Emphasis on Relapse Prevention

Relapse is a common concern for individuals in recovery from both mental health disorders and addiction. Developing effective relapse prevention strategies is essential. These strategies often involve identifying triggers, building healthy coping mechanisms, and learning to manage stress and negative emotions in healthier ways. Regular therapy sessions and ongoing support from mental health professionals can play a significant role in preventing relapse.

Conclusion

The intricate relationship between mental health disorders and addiction necessitates a comprehensive and holistic approach to treatment and recovery. Acknowledging the shared vulnerabilities, understanding the neurobiological connections, and addressing the role of trauma are critical steps in breaking the cycle of dual diagnosis. By integrating various therapeutic modalities, fostering support networks, and prioritizing relapse prevention, individuals can overcome the challenges posed by mental health disorders and addiction, ultimately reclaiming their lives and achieving lasting recovery.

Introduction

Addiction, whether to smoking, alcohol, or drugs, exerts a profound toll on both the mind and the body. This chapter delves into the intricate relationship between addiction and physical health, focusing on the dire consequences that these substances inflict on various physiological systems. From respiratory issues to liver damage and more, the harmful effects of addiction are far-reaching and demand attention. By understanding the intricate ways in which addiction affects the body, individuals can gain insight into the imperative to overcome these habits for the sake of their long-term well-being.

The Respiratory System: A Struggle to Breathe

1. Smoking and Respiratory Compromises

Tobacco smoking, a prevalent addiction, significantly impacts the respiratory system. The inhalation of harmful chemicals such as nicotine and tar directly affects the lungs, leading to issues like chronic obstructive pulmonary disease (COPD) and lung cancer. The tiny air sacs in the lungs, known as alveoli, become damaged and lose their elasticity, leading to breathing difficulties and reduced lung capacity. COPD, characterized by chronic bronchitis and emphysema, is a slow and progressive disease that severely hampers lung function, making even simple tasks like climbing stairs a challenge.

While the impact of drugs and alcohol on the respiratory system might not be as direct as smoking, their consequences are noteworthy. Opioids, for instance, can depress the respiratory center in the brain, slowing down breathing to dangerous levels. Similarly, excessive alcohol consumption can weaken the muscles responsible for maintaining a clear airway, increasing the risk of conditions like sleep apnea. Prolonged drug or alcohol abuse can compromise overall lung health and increase vulnerability to infections like pneumonia.

Ravaging the Liver: Alcohol and Drug Induced Damage

1. The Liver's Role and Vulnerability

The liver is a vital organ responsible for detoxification, metabolism, and nutrient storage. However, addiction to alcohol and drugs subjects the liver to immense stress. Alcohol, when consumed excessively, overwhelms the liver's ability to process it, leading to fatty liver disease, alcoholic hepatitis, and ultimately, cirrhosis. Cirrhosis is the late stage of scarring of the liver tissue and can lead to liver failure, necessitating a transplant for survival.

2. Drugs and the Liver

Drug addiction is equally detrimental to the liver. Injected drugs, for instance, can introduce harmful contaminants into the bloodstream, putting additional stress on the liver's detoxification processes. Additionally, certain drugs can directly damage liver cells, leading to conditions like drug-induced hepatitis. Sharing needles during drug use further exacerbates the risk of contracting bloodborne infections like hepatitis B and C, further compromising liver health.

Cardiovascular Complications: Strain on the Heart

1. Smoking's Impact on the Heart

The cardiovascular system is profoundly affected by addiction, particularly in the case of smoking. Nicotine, a highly addictive component of tobacco, raises blood pressure and increases heart rate, putting undue stress on the heart. Over time, this can lead to atherosclerosis, a condition where fatty deposits accumulate in the arteries, narrowing them and restricting blood flow. Ultimately, this can result in heart attacks, strokes, and other cardiovascular diseases.

2. Alcohol, Drugs, and Heart Health

Alcohol abuse also takes a toll on the cardiovascular system. Chronic alcohol consumption can weaken the heart muscle, leading to cardiomyopathy, a condition where the heart becomes enlarged and less efficient in pumping blood. Illicit drugs like cocaine can have an acute impact, causing heart palpitations, chest pain, and even fatal arrhythmias. The combination of these substances with compromised heart function is a recipe for catastrophic health events.

Neurological Woes: Impact on the Nervous System

1. The Pleasure Pathway and Addiction

Addictive substances often target the brain's reward system, flooding it with dopamine and creating feelings of euphoria. However, prolonged substance abuse can lead to neuroadaptation, where the brain becomes accustomed to the excess dopamine and reduces its natural production.

This results in a diminished response to pleasurable stimuli and a higher tolerance for the addictive substance, leading to a vicious cycle of increased consumption.

2. Nervous System Vulnerability

The nervous system bears the brunt of addiction's impact, as drugs and alcohol can disrupt its delicate balance. Chronic drug use can damage neurons and impair cognitive function, leading to memory problems, decreased decision-making abilities, and altered behavior. Alcohol, a depressant, can dampen nerve impulses, leading to coordination issues and slowed reflexes. Additionally, addiction can increase susceptibility to mental health disorders, creating a complex interplay between substance abuse and mental well-being.

Renal Consequences: Kidney Function Impairment

Filtering Toxins: Kidneys Under Strain

The kidneys play a crucial role in filtering toxins from the bloodstream and regulating fluid balance. However, addiction can overwhelm these organs and compromise their function. Both alcohol and certain drugs can cause high blood pressure, leading to chronic kidney disease. Additionally, substances like heroin can directly damage kidney tissues, impairing their ability to filter waste efficiently. Without proper kidney function, toxins accumulate in the body, leading to a host of health complications.

Conclusion

The physical health consequences of addiction are undeniable and far-reaching. From the respiratory system to the cardiovascular, nervous, and renal systems, the toll taken by substances like smoking, alcohol, and drugs is profound. The effects are not limited to a single organ; rather, they create a cascade of interrelated issues that can significantly decrease quality of life and, in extreme cases, result in premature death.

However, understanding the intricate ways in which addiction affects the body can serve as a powerful motivator for individuals to seek help and embark on the journey of recovery. Overcoming addiction requires addressing both the physical and psychological aspects of dependence. By prioritizing one's well-being and seeking professional support, individuals can mitigate the damage caused by addiction and begin the process of healing.

Ultimately, the road to recovery is challenging, but it offers the promise of renewed health, vitality, and a chance for a better future. It is never too late to take the first step toward overcoming addiction and reclaiming control over one's physical and mental well-being.

Introduction

Addiction is a complex and multifaceted issue that often intertwines with various mental health conditions. In this chapter, we will delve into the intricate relationship between addiction and conditions such as anxiety, depression, and psychosis. Understanding these connections is crucial for designing effective strategies to overcome substance addiction while also addressing the mental health challenges that often accompany it.

The Vicious Cycle: Addiction and Mental Health

1. Dual Diagnosis: The Co-Occurrence of Addiction and Mental Health Disorders

The co-occurrence of addiction and mental health disorders, commonly referred to as dual diagnosis or comorbidity, is a well-documented phenomenon. Studies have consistently shown that individuals struggling with addiction are more likely to experience conditions like anxiety, depression, and psychosis. This raises the question: Is addiction a cause or an effect of these mental health conditions?

2. The Bidirectional Relationship

The relationship between addiction and mental health is bidirectional. On one hand, substance abuse can lead to or exacerbate mental health issues. Drugs and alcohol can disrupt brain chemistry, leading to imbalances that trigger symptoms of anxiety, depression, and even psychosis. On the other hand, individuals with pre-existing mental health conditions might turn to substances as a way to self-medicate and alleviate their symptoms temporarily. This dual dynamic complicates treatment strategies, emphasizing the need for a holistic approach that addresses both addiction and mental health.

Anxiety and Addiction: A Tangled Web

1. The Anxiety-Substance Connection

Anxiety and addiction often go hand in hand, forming a complex interplay that can reinforce each other's effects. Those suffering from anxiety disorders may turn to substances as a way to cope with their overwhelming feelings of fear and unease. The immediate relief provided by drugs or alcohol can create a dangerous cycle of reliance.

2. The Brain Chemistry Perspective

Neurologically, chronic substance abuse can alter the brain's reward pathways and stress response systems, which are closely tied to anxiety disorders. As a result, individuals can become more prone to developing anxiety-related conditions as their substance use continues.

3. Treatment Approaches

Treating co-occurring anxiety and addiction requires addressing both issues concurrently. Cognitive-behavioral therapies, support groups, and medication can play vital roles in breaking the cycle and providing healthier coping mechanisms for anxiety.

Depression's Grip: Exploring the Depths of Addiction

1. Self-Medication and Escapism

Depression's debilitating weight can drive individuals toward substance abuse as a form of self-medication. Drugs and alcohol can momentarily alleviate feelings of emptiness and sadness, offering a fleeting sense of pleasure or distraction.

2. The Neurochemical Dance

Depression and addiction share common neural pathways, particularly those involving dopamine and serotonin. Substance use can disrupt these neurotransmitter systems, leading to worsened depressive symptoms over time.

3. Seeking Light: Recovery Strategies

To address the intertwining challenges of depression and addiction, a comprehensive approach is necessary. Therapy, lifestyle changes, and, when appropriate, medication, can help individuals navigate the path to recovery, rebuilding their mental health in the process.

Psychosis and Substance Abuse: Navigating Reality

1. Unraveling the Connection

Psychosis, characterized by a disconnection from reality, can be exacerbated by substance abuse. Drugs such as hallucinogens or stimulants can trigger or intensify psychotic episodes, making it crucial to examine the relationship between these two complex phenomena.

Distinguishing between substance-induced psychosis and primary psychotic disorders is a diagnostic challenge. Substance-induced psychosis is temporary and usually resolves with abstinence, whereas primary psychosis stems from underlying mental health conditions.

When addressing co-occurring psychosis and substance abuse, a comprehensive assessment is vital. Treatment may involve medical detoxification, antipsychotic medications, psychotherapy, and ongoing support to ensure stability and recovery.

Holistic Healing: Integrated Treatment Approaches

To effectively address addiction and its intertwined mental health challenges, an integrated approach is essential. Isolating treatment for addiction or mental health in isolation often leads to incomplete recovery.

Specialized dual diagnosis treatment programs are designed to tackle both addiction and mental health disorders simultaneously. These programs offer a range of therapeutic interventions, including individual and group therapy, psychiatric care, and educational workshops.

Support systems, including family, friends, and community, play a pivotal role in the recovery journey. Open conversations and understanding can help individuals feel less isolated and more motivated to seek help.

Conclusion

The relationship between addiction and mental health conditions like anxiety, depression, and psychosis is undeniably complex. As we've explored in this chapter, these connections are often bidirectional, with each influencing and exacerbating the other. Addressing addiction while neglecting the associated mental health challenges is a short-sighted approach. Instead, a comprehensive strategy that acknowledges the interconnectedness of these issues is necessary for successful recovery. By embracing integrated treatments, fostering support systems, and promoting mental health awareness, we can offer individuals struggling with addiction a genuine chance at overcoming their challenges and rebuilding their lives.

Introduction

Addiction to smoking, alcohol, and drugs is a pervasive problem that affects millions of individuals worldwide. Breaking free from the grasp of addiction requires a multifaceted approach that addresses both the physical and psychological aspects of dependence. In this chapter, we delve into the various treatment options available to those seeking to overcome their addiction. From therapy to medication to rehabilitation programs, we explore the approaches that offer hope and healing to individuals on their journey to recovery.

Therapeutic Interventions

1. Cognitive Behavioral Therapy (CBT)

Cognitive Behavioral Therapy, often abbreviated as CBT, is a widely recognized and effective therapeutic approach for addiction treatment. This evidence-based method focuses on identifying and modifying negative thought patterns and behaviors that contribute to addiction. CBT helps individuals develop healthier coping strategies, enhance self-awareness, and manage triggers that lead to substance use. Through regular sessions with a trained therapist, clients learn to reframe their perceptions and build resilience against relapse.

2. Motivational Interviewing

Motivational Interviewing (MI) is a client-centered counseling technique that aims to enhance an individual's motivation to change addictive behaviors. Therapists using

MI create a supportive and non-confrontational environment to explore the individual's ambivalence towards quitting substances. By fostering intrinsic motivation and self-efficacy, MI empowers clients to set achievable goals and make positive changes in their lives. This approach is particularly effective in the early stages of recovery when individuals may be unsure about committing to treatment.

3. Group Therapy

Group therapy provides a platform for individuals to share their experiences, struggles, and successes with others facing similar challenges. Led by a trained therapist, group therapy sessions offer a sense of belonging and camaraderie. Participants receive encouragement, empathy, and insights from peers, fostering a strong support network. Group therapy not only promotes emotional healing but also provides an opportunity to learn from others' coping strategies and relapse prevention techniques.

Medication-Assisted Treatment

1. NRT and Medications for Smoking Cessation

Nicotine Replacement Therapy (NRT) is a common approach for individuals seeking to quit smoking. NRT involves using products like nicotine gum, patches, or lozenges to gradually reduce nicotine dependence while managing withdrawal symptoms. Additionally, prescription medications such as bupropion and varenicline can help curb cravings and reduce the pleasure derived from smoking. Combining medication with behavioral therapy can significantly improve smoking cessation outcomes.

2. Medications for Alcohol Use Disorder

Medications have been developed to assist individuals in overcoming alcohol use disorder. Disulfiram, for example, creates adverse reactions when alcohol is consumed, acting as a deterrent. Naltrexone and acamprosate work by reducing cravings and minimizing the pleasurable effects of alcohol. These medications, when prescribed and monitored by a medical professional, can be valuable tools in achieving sobriety.

3. Medications for Opioid and Drug Addiction

Opioid addiction can be particularly challenging to overcome due to the intense withdrawal symptoms and cravings. Medications like methadone, buprenorphine, and naltrexone help manage these challenges. Methadone and buprenorphine are opioid agonists that reduce withdrawal symptoms, while naltrexone blocks the effects of opioids, discouraging their use. Similar medication-assisted treatments exist for other drug addictions, aiding individuals in stabilizing their lives and reducing the risk of relapse.

Rehabilitation Programs

1. Inpatient Rehabilitation

Inpatient rehabilitation, also known as residential treatment, offers a structured and immersive environment for individuals seeking to overcome addiction. Clients reside at the treatment facility, receiving round-the-clock care and support. Inpatient programs provide a safe space to detoxify, undergo therapy, and develop essential life skills for a drug-free future. These programs are particularly beneficial for those with severe addictions, as they remove individuals from triggering environments and offer intensive therapeutic interventions.

2. Outpatient Rehabilitation

Outpatient rehabilitation programs allow individuals to receive treatment while continuing to live at home. This flexibility is advantageous for those with milder addictions or significant personal responsibilities. Outpatient programs involve regular therapy sessions, group meetings, and skill-building workshops. However, individuals in outpatient treatment must have a strong support system in place to navigate potential triggers in their everyday lives.

3. Holistic and Alternative Rehabilitation

Holistic and alternative rehabilitation programs focus on treating the whole person - mind, body, and spirit. These programs incorporate a range of therapies such as yoga, meditation, art therapy, and nutritional counseling. By addressing the physical, emotional, and spiritual aspects of addiction, holistic programs aim to promote overall well-being and equip individuals with tools to manage stress and triggers.

Conclusion

Overcoming addiction to smoking, alcohol, and drugs requires a combination of approaches tailored to the individual's unique needs. Therapy helps individuals understand the root causes of their addiction and develop healthier coping strategies. Medications can alleviate withdrawal symptoms and cravings, making the journey to recovery more manageable. Rehabilitation programs provide the necessary structure and support for individuals to rebuild their lives free from addiction.

It's important to note that there is no one-size-fits-all solution to addiction treatment. The most effective approach often involves a combination of therapies and interventions. With the right support, individuals can embark on a path of healing, rediscovering their strengths and regaining control over their lives. Whether it's through therapy, medication, or rehabilitation programs, hope shines bright for those who are committed to breaking free from the cycle of addiction.

Introduction

Smoking addiction is a global concern that affects millions of lives, leading to various health complications and diminishing the overall quality of life. However, the journey to quitting smoking is often filled with challenges, triggers, and setbacks. In this chapter, we will explore effective strategies, practical tips, and inspiring success stories that can empower individuals to overcome smoking addiction. By understanding the psychological and physiological aspects of addiction, as well as adopting proven techniques, smokers can take meaningful steps towards a smoke-free life.

Understanding Smoking Addiction

The Complex Nature of Nicotine Addiction

Nicotine, a highly addictive substance present in cigarettes, hooks individuals by affecting the brain's reward system. This leads to cravings and withdrawal symptoms when trying to quit. Recognizing nicotine's grip on the body and mind is crucial for devising successful quitting strategies.

Building the Foundation for Success

1. Setting Clear Goals

Quitting smoking starts with a clear and achievable goal. Setting a quit date and establishing reasons for quitting can provide a strong motivational foundation.

2. Understanding Triggers

Identifying triggers that prompt smoking can help individuals anticipate and manage cravings. Triggers may include stress, social situations, or specific locations.

3. Gathering Support

Having a support network can make a significant difference. Inform friends, family, and coworkers about the quit plan, and consider joining support groups or seeking professional counseling.

Strategies for Quitting Smoking

1. Cold Turkey

Quitting abruptly, also known as going "cold turkey," involves immediate cessation without any nicotine replacement. While challenging, this approach works for individuals who prefer a swift break from their habit.

2. Nicotine Replacement Therapy (NRT)

NRT involves using products like nicotine gum, patches, lozenges, or inhalers to gradually reduce nicotine intake. This helps manage withdrawal symptoms and cravings during the quitting process.

3. Behavioral Therapy

Cognitive-behavioral therapy (CBT) can assist in identifying and altering thought patterns associated with smoking. This approach equips individuals with coping mechanisms for cravings and stress.

4. Medications

Certain prescription medications, such as varenicline and bupropion, can aid in quitting by reducing cravings and withdrawal symptoms. Consult a healthcare professional to determine the best medication for individual needs.

5. Alternative Therapies

Practices like acupuncture, mindfulness meditation, and yoga have shown promise in supporting smoking cessation. These techniques promote relaxation and stress reduction.

Tips for Success

1. Find Healthy Substitutes

Replace smoking with healthier alternatives like chewing sugar-free gum, snacking on fruits and vegetables, or engaging in physical activities.

2. Practice Stress Management

Stress often triggers cravings. Engage in activities that reduce stress, such as exercise, deep breathing, or engaging hobbies.

3. Modify Routine and Environment

Adjust daily routines to avoid situations that trigger smoking. Rearrange living spaces to remove smoking cues and reminders.

4. Reward Milestones

Celebrate milestones along the journey. Use the money saved from not buying cigarettes to treat yourself to something enjoyable.

Inspiring Success Stories

1. Sarah's Journey to Smoke-Free Living

Sarah, a longtime smoker, decided to quit after her daughter expressed concern about her health. She combined NRT with regular exercise and found solace in journaling during cravings. Sarah's determination led her to a smoke-free life, and she now enjoys outdoor activities with her daughter.

2. Mark: Overcoming Decades of Addiction

Mark had been smoking for over three decades. With the support of a smoking cessation group, he gradually reduced his nicotine intake using patches. Mark's success inspired him to become a counselor, helping others achieve their smoke-free goals.

Conclusion

Overcoming smoking addiction requires dedication, patience, and a combination of strategies tailored to individual preferences. By understanding the nature of nicotine addiction, building a strong foundation, adopting proven techniques, and seeking support, smokers can take control of their lives and embark on a journey towards improved health and well-being. The success stories of individuals like Sarah and Mark serve as beacons of hope, reminding us that with determination and the right tools, a smoke-free life is achievable for anyone. Remember, it's never too late to break free from smoking addiction and embrace a brighter, healthier future.

Introduction

Alcohol addiction, also known as alcoholism, is a pervasive and complex issue that affects millions of individuals worldwide. Overcoming alcohol addiction requires a multifaceted approach that encompasses not only physical detoxification but also psychological healing, support systems, and strategies to prevent relapse. This chapter delves into the intricacies of recovery from alcohol addiction, exploring the recovery process, the importance of support systems, and effective methods for relapse prevention.

The Recovery Process: A Multidimensional Journey

Recovering from alcohol addiction is a challenging and gradual process that involves several stages. It's essential to recognize that recovery is not linear; setbacks can occur, but they do not define the overall journey.

1. Acknowledgment and Acceptance

The first step towards recovery is acknowledging the presence of alcohol addiction and accepting the need for change. This stage often involves introspection, as individuals confront the impact of their addiction on their lives and the lives of those around them.

2. Detoxification

Once an individual decides to pursue recovery, the physical aspect of addiction is addressed through detoxification. This process allows the body to rid itself of alcohol and its toxins. Medical supervision is crucial during this stage, as withdrawal symptoms can be severe and even life-threatening.

3. Therapeutic Intervention

Recovery from alcohol addiction involves a significant psychological component. Therapeutic interventions, such as individual counseling, group therapy, and cognitive-behavioral therapy (CBT), help individuals understand the underlying causes of their addiction and develop coping mechanisms to manage triggers.

4. Building a Support Network

Isolation can hinder recovery progress. Establishing a strong support network is vital. This network may include family, friends, support groups, and mental health professionals. These individuals provide encouragement, understanding, and a sense of accountability.

5. Lifestyle Changes

Recovery necessitates making positive changes in various areas of life. Adopting a healthy lifestyle through proper nutrition, regular exercise, and sufficient sleep contributes to physical and mental well-being, reducing the risk of relapse.

6. Setting Goals and Finding Purpose

Recovery becomes more meaningful when individuals set goals for themselves. These goals can be related to career, education, relationships, or personal growth. Having a sense of purpose can boost self-esteem and motivation.

7. Continued Self-Care and Maintenance

Recovery is an ongoing process that requires continuous self-care and maintenance. Attending support group meetings, staying connected with the support network, and engaging in activities that bring joy and fulfillment are crucial for sustained recovery.

The Importance of Support Systems

Recovering from alcohol addiction is not a journey that can be undertaken alone. Support systems play a pivotal role in providing encouragement, guidance, and a sense of belonging.

1. Family and Friends

The support of family and friends can significantly impact the recovery process. Their understanding, empathy, and non-judgmental attitude create a safe space for individuals to share their struggles and triumphs.

2. Support Groups

Support groups, such as Alcoholics Anonymous (AA), provide a platform for individuals in recovery to connect with others who have faced similar challenges. These groups offer a sense of community, where members share their experiences, offer advice, and celebrate milestones.

3. Therapists and Counselors

Mental health professionals specializing in addiction can guide individuals through the emotional complexities of recovery. Therapists and counselors offer strategies to cope with cravings, address underlying emotional issues, and develop effective relapse prevention plans.

4. Structured Treatment Programs

Inpatient or outpatient treatment programs offer structured environments for recovery. These programs combine medical supervision, therapy, and education to equip individuals with the tools needed to maintain sobriety.

5. Online Resources

The digital age has brought forth online support communities and resources. Websites, forums, and apps dedicated to recovery provide a convenient way to connect with others, access information, and find inspiration.

Preventing Relapse: Strategies for Long-Term Sobriety

Relapse is a common concern during the recovery journey. Preventing relapse requires a combination of self-awareness, coping skills, and proactive measures.

1. Identifying Triggers

Recognizing triggers that can lead to alcohol cravings is essential. Triggers can be emotional, environmental, or social. Common triggers include stress, negative emotions, certain social settings, and exposure to alcohol.

2. Developing Coping Mechanisms

Coping mechanisms are healthy strategies to manage triggers and cravings. Techniques such as deep breathing, mindfulness meditation, engaging in hobbies, and reaching out to a support network can help individuals navigate challenging situations.

3. Creating a Relapse Prevention Plan

A relapse prevention plan outlines specific steps to take if cravings become overwhelming. It includes contact information for support individuals, coping strategies, and reminders of the reasons for pursuing sobriety.

4. Learning from Setbacks

If a relapse does occur, it's essential to view it as a setback rather than a failure. Individuals can learn from the experience, identify what led to the relapse, and adjust their strategies accordingly.

5. Mindfulness and Self-Care

Practicing mindfulness involves staying present and aware of one's thoughts, emotions, and physical sensations. This practice can enhance self-awareness and help individuals make conscious choices that support their recovery.

Conclusion

Recovering from alcohol addiction is a transformative journey that requires commitment, resilience, and the support of a robust network. The recovery process encompasses acknowledging the problem, addressing physical and psychological aspects, building a support system, and developing relapse prevention strategies. While the path to recovery is undoubtedly challenging, it's also one of growth, self-discovery, and the regaining of control over one's life. By understanding the recovery process, harnessing the power of support systems, and implementing effective relapse prevention techniques, individuals can achieve long-term sobriety and embrace a healthier, more fulfilling life.

Introduction

In the realm of substance abuse, drug addiction stands as one of the most complex and challenging issues individuals can face. The journey from addiction to sobriety is not a linear path but rather a multifaceted process filled with obstacles and triumphs. This chapter delves into the intricacies of managing drug addiction, examining the challenges inherent in overcoming addiction and the strategies required to maintain lasting sobriety.

Understanding the Nature of Drug Addiction

1. The Brain and Reward Pathways

Drug addiction is rooted in the brain's intricate reward pathways. When individuals consume drugs, these substances flood the brain with dopamine, creating intense feelings of pleasure and euphoria. Over time, the brain adapts to this flood of dopamine, leading to tolerance and the need for increasing amounts of the drug to achieve the same effect.

2. Psychological and Physical Dependence

Drug addiction is a two-fold challenge encompassing both psychological and physical dependence. Psychological dependence involves the emotional and mental reliance on the drug to cope with stress, emotions, and life's challenges. Physical dependence, on the other hand, manifests through withdrawal symptoms when the drug is not consumed. These symptoms can be intensely uncomfortable and can range from nausea and tremors to seizures and hallucinations.

The Challenges of Overcoming Drug Addiction

1. Withdrawal Symptoms and Cravings

The early stages of overcoming drug addiction are often marked by withdrawal symptoms and intense cravings. These symptoms can be both physically and emotionally debilitating, pushing individuals back into drug use as a means of relief. Navigating this phase requires a strong support system and coping strategies to manage the discomfort.

2. Underlying Psychological Factors

Many individuals turn to drugs as a way to self-medicate underlying psychological issues such as anxiety, depression, trauma, or stress. Overcoming addiction involves addressing these root causes, which often necessitates professional therapeutic intervention. Unpacking these psychological factors is crucial for sustained recovery.

3. Social and Environmental Triggers

External triggers, including social circles and environmental cues, can pose significant challenges to sobriety. Being in the presence of old friends who still use drugs or returning to environments associated with drug use can evoke powerful cravings. Learning to navigate these triggers is an essential aspect of managing drug addiction.

Strategies for Overcoming Drug Addiction

1. Professional Treatment Options

Seeking professional help is often the cornerstone of overcoming drug addiction. Treatment options include:

Inpatient Rehabilitation

Inpatient rehab facilities offer a structured and supervised environment for individuals to detox and receive intensive therapy. This option removes individuals from triggering environments and provides round-the-clock support.

Outpatient Programs

Outpatient programs allow individuals to receive treatment while living at home. These programs provide flexibility for those who need to maintain work, family, or educational commitments.

Therapy and Counseling

Therapeutic interventions, such as cognitive-behavioral therapy (CBT) and dialectical behavior therapy (DBT), help individuals understand the thought patterns and behaviors driving their addiction. Counseling equips individuals with coping mechanisms and life skills to navigate triggers and stressors.

2. Peer Support and Community

Engaging with support groups, such as Narcotics Anonymous (NA) https://www.na.org/ or SMART Recovery https://www.smartrecovery.org/ connects individuals with peers who are also on the journey to sobriety. These groups provide a safe space to share experiences, setbacks, and successes, reducing feelings of isolation.

3. Holistic Approaches

Holistic approaches focus on healing the mind, body, and spirit. These may include practices such as yoga, meditation, art therapy, and mindfulness. Engaging in these activities fosters self-awareness, reduces stress, and aids in managing cravings.

Maintaining Sobriety: Long-Term Strategies

1. Developing a Strong Support Network

Maintaining sobriety requires ongoing support. This includes building a network of friends, family, mentors, and support groups. Surrounding oneself with positive influences enhances accountability and provides a safety net during challenging times.

2. Healthy Lifestyle Choices

Adopting a healthy lifestyle can significantly contribute to long-term sobriety. Regular exercise, balanced nutrition, and adequate sleep improve physical and mental well-being, reducing the risk of relapse.

3. Setting Realistic Goals

Goal-setting provides a sense of purpose and direction in recovery. Setting achievable short-term and long-term goals boosts self-esteem and motivation. Celebrating milestones, no matter how small, reinforces the progress made.

4. Stress Management Techniques

Stress is a common trigger for relapse. Learning effective stress management techniques such as deep breathing, progressive muscle relaxation, and time management helps individuals navigate life's challenges without resorting to drugs.

5. Avoiding High-Risk Situations

Identifying and avoiding high-risk situations and triggers is essential for maintaining sobriety. This might involve distancing oneself from certain people, places, or activities that are associated with drug use.

6. Continued Therapy and Aftercare

Recovery is an ongoing process. Continued therapy, counseling, or participation in aftercare programs helps individuals stay focused on their sobriety goals. These resources provide a space to address new challenges that arise in the post-recovery phase.

Conclusion

Managing drug addiction is a journey that demands dedication, resilience, and a multifaceted approach. Overcoming addiction involves addressing the physical and psychological aspects of dependence while navigating challenges such as withdrawal symptoms, triggers, and social pressures. With professional treatment, peer support, and holistic strategies, individuals can transition into a life of sobriety. The key to maintaining this sobriety lies in developing a strong support network, adopting healthy habits, managing stress, and continuing therapy. As we strive to understand the complexities of addiction, it is imperative to provide individuals with the tools and knowledge they need to triumph over the challenges and achieve lasting recovery.

Introduction

Addiction is a complex and challenging issue that not only affects the individual struggling with it but also has a profound impact on their family members and loved ones. Watching someone you care about battle with addiction can be heart-wrenching and overwhelming. However, family support can play a crucial role in the recovery journey. This chapter aims to provide practical guidance for family members and loved ones on how to offer effective support to those facing addiction.

Understanding Addiction

Before delving into the strategies for supporting someone struggling with addiction, it's important to understand the nature of addiction itself. Addiction is a chronic disease that affects the brain's reward system, leading to compulsive behavior and the inability to control the use of substances. It's characterized by physical, psychological, and behavioral symptoms.

Overcoming Stigma and Judgment

One of the first steps family members and loved ones can take is to overcome any stigma or judgment associated with addiction. Addiction is a medical condition, not a moral failing. Avoiding blame and negative language can create a more conducive environment for open communication and healing.

Educating Yourself about Addiction

Families can better support their loved ones by educating themselves about addiction. Understanding the underlying causes, triggers, and the science behind addiction can help family members approach the situation with empathy and knowledge. Various resources, such as books, articles, and support groups, provide valuable insights into addiction's complexities.

Open and Non-judgmental Communication

Effective communication is key when dealing with addiction. Creating a safe space for open and non-judgmental conversations encourages the individual struggling with addiction to share their feelings and experiences. Active listening and empathy are essential during these discussions.

Encouraging Professional Help

While family support is vital, addiction often requires professional intervention. Encourage your loved one to seek help from healthcare professionals, therapists, or addiction specialists. Offering to assist in finding suitable treatment options and accompanying them to appointments can demonstrate your commitment to their recovery.

Setting Boundaries and Providing Tough Love

Supporting someone with addiction doesn't mean enabling their destructive behavior. Setting healthy boundaries is essential for both the individual and the family's well-being. While it can be difficult, interventions such as "tough love" may be necessary to motivate the person to seek help. It's important to strike a balance between support and accountability.

Avoiding Enabling Behaviors

Enabling behaviors inadvertently perpetuate the cycle of addiction. This can include providing financial support that fuels the addiction, making excuses for the person's behavior, or shielding them from the consequences of their actions. Recognizing and refraining from enabling behaviors is critical for the person's recovery journey.

Attending Family Therapy

Addiction doesn't just affect the individual; it impacts the entire family dynamic. Family therapy can provide a platform for family members to address their own emotions, challenges, and misunderstandings. It also fosters understanding of the addicted person's struggles and promotes healing for everyone involved.

Practicing Self-Care

Supporting someone with addiction can take a toll on your emotional and mental well-being. Engaging in regular self-care activities, such as exercise, hobbies, and spending time with supportive friends, is essential for maintaining your own health. When you take care of yourself, you're better equipped to provide meaningful support.

Celebrating Progress

Recovery from addiction is a journey with its ups and downs. Celebrate the small victories along the way – whether it's completing a counseling session, staying sober for a week, or achieving a personal goal. Positive reinforcement boosts morale and reinforces the individual's commitment to their recovery.

Patience and Understanding

Recovery from addiction is not a linear process. There will be setbacks and relapses, but these don't define the person's journey. Patience and understanding are crucial during these challenging times. Avoid expressing disappointment or frustration, and instead, offer reassurance and a renewed focus on moving forward.

Dealing with Relapse

Relapses are often part of the recovery process, and they can be disheartening for both the individual and their family. It's important to approach relapse with empathy and without blame. Encourage your loved one to learn from the experience, seek professional help if needed, and continue their journey to recovery.

Connecting with Support Groups

Support groups provide a sense of community and understanding that can be incredibly valuable for both the person in recovery and their family members. These groups offer a platform to share experiences, coping strategies, and success stories. Many families find solace in knowing they are not alone in their challenges.

Never Giving Up

Supporting a loved one through addiction requires unwavering dedication. There may be moments of frustration and hopelessness, but never give up on your loved one's potential to overcome addiction. Your support, love, and belief in their ability to recover can make a significant difference in their journey.

Conclusion

Supporting someone struggling with addiction is a journey that requires compassion, patience, and understanding. As a family member or loved one, your role is pivotal in creating an environment that fosters recovery. By educating yourself, communicating effectively, and offering the right balance of support and accountability, you can be a beacon of hope in your loved one's path toward overcoming addiction. Remember that addiction recovery is possible, and your unwavering support can be a guiding light in their darkest moments.

Introduction

Addiction recovery is a challenging journey that often requires a combination of personal determination, professional assistance, and community support. Individuals grappling with smoking, alcohol, or drug addiction need access to reliable information, guidance, and encouragement. Fortunately, there is a wide range of organizations, hotlines, and online platforms that offer crucial resources to aid in the recovery process. This chapter explores a variety of these community resources available globally, including specific options for individuals in India.

International Resources

1. Alcoholics Anonymous (AA)

Alcoholics Anonymous, a globally recognized organization, provides a supportive community for individuals struggling with alcohol addiction. AA offers regular meetings, both in person and online, where members share their experiences, strengths, and hopes. The organization's 12-step program is designed to help individuals achieve and maintain sobriety. The official website https://www.aa.org/ provides information about meetings, literature, and resources.

2. Narcotics Anonymous (NA)

Similar to AA, Narcotics Anonymous focuses on supporting individuals recovering from drug addiction. NA's program is centered around a 12-step model that encourages members to admit their powerlessness over addiction and seek spiritual growth. Their website https://www.na.org/ offers meeting information, literature, and online discussion forums.

3. SMART Recovery

SMART Recovery offers a science-based approach to addiction recovery, utilizing cognitive-behavioral techniques and motivational enhancement strategies. Their global community provides both in-person and online meetings, encouraging participants to develop self-empowerment and coping skills. The official website https://www.smartrecovery.org/ offers tools, resources, and a forum for support.

4. In The Rooms

In The Rooms is an online platform that hosts virtual recovery meetings for various types of addiction, including smoking, alcohol, and drug addiction. With a diverse range of meetings available 24/7, individuals can find support and connection from the comfort of their own homes. The website https://www.intherooms.com/ also features a social network for members to connect and share.

Resources in the United States

1. National Helpline

The Substance Abuse and Mental Health Services Administration (SAMHSA) operates a confidential and free National Helpline (1-800-662-HELP) available 24/7. Trained professionals offer assistance in English and Spanish, providing information, resources, and referrals to local treatment facilities. Please refer their website https://www.samhsa.gov/ .

2. National Institute on Drug Abuse (NIDA)

NIDA, a part of the National Institutes of Health, offers a wealth of research-based information about addiction, treatment options, and recovery. Their website https://nida.nih.gov/ includes educational resources, publications, and tools for individuals, families, and healthcare professionals.

3. Quitline

For those looking to quit smoking, the National Cancer Institute operates a Smoking Quitline (1-877-44U-QUIT) that provides support and resources tailored to each individual's needs. The helpline assists smokers in creating personalized quit plans and offers assistance in multiple languages.

Resources in India

1. Alcoholics Anonymous India

AA has a presence in India, with local chapters offering meetings and support groups across various cities. These groups provide a space for individuals to share their struggles and progress in a culturally relevant context. Information about AA meetings in India can be found on the global AA website https://www.aa.org/ or through local listings.

2. The Banyan

Based in Chennai, The Banyan focuses on supporting individuals dealing with mental health and substance abuse issues. Their holistic approach includes medical care, counseling, and community reintegration. The organization's efforts are particularly geared towards marginalized populations. Please refer their website https://thebanyan.org/ .

3. Kripa Foundation

Kripa Foundation operates in several states across India, providing rehabilitation and support services for individuals dealing with addiction. They offer residential treatment, counseling, and aftercare services, aiming to help individuals reintegrate into society as productive members. Please refer their website https://kripafoundation.org/ .

International Online Communities

1. Soberistas

Soberistas is an online community that extends its support to individuals worldwide. It provides a platform for people to share their stories, connect with others, and find inspiration on their journey to recovery. The website https://soberistas.com/ features forums, blogs, and a supportive network for those seeking sobriety.

2. SoberRecovery

SoberRecovery is a comprehensive online resource https://www.soberrecovery.com/ offering forums, articles, and information on addiction recovery. With a global user base, individuals can connect, seek advice, and find encouragement from others who understand their struggles.

Online Platforms in the United States

1. Heroes in Recovery

Heroes in Recovery is an online platform https://heroesinrecovery.com/ in the United States that encourages individuals to share their stories of recovery, resilience, and hope. The website features personal narratives, articles, and resources for those on their path to overcoming addiction.

2. In The Rooms

In addition to its global reach, In The Rooms https://www.intherooms.com/ offers a space for individuals in the United States to connect online, attend virtual meetings, and access resources specific to their region. The platform serves as a bridge for local and international recovery communities.

Conclusion

Overcoming smoking, alcohol, and drug addiction requires a multifaceted approach that includes personal determination, professional assistance, and community support. The resources listed in this chapter provide a starting point for individuals seeking help on their journey to recovery. From internationally recognized organizations like AA and NA to country-specific initiatives, these community resources serve as beacons of hope, guiding individuals toward healthier, addiction-free lives. Remember, reaching out for support is a sign of strength, and the path to recovery is one that no one has to walk alone.

"Overcoming Smoking, Alcohol, and Drug Addiction" is an insightful guide that comprehensively addresses the complex journey of breaking free from addiction. It begins by elucidating the profound impact of addiction on individuals and society. Delving into the Science of Addiction, it uncovers the intricate neurological and psychological underpinnings of this struggle. The book adeptly navigates through specific addictions - Smoking, Alcohol, and Drugs - elucidating their allure, effects, and challenges in separate chapters.

Genetic Predisposition and Environmental Factors are scrutinized for their roles, while Psychological Factors are dissected for their contribution to the cycle. The book meticulously unravels the harrowing consequences addiction inflicts on physical health and mental well-being. With remarkable clarity, it outlines diverse therapeutic approaches and interventions as Approaches to Treatment. Practical solutions and motivating triumphs are shared for conquering smoking, alcohol, and drug addiction individually. Recovery methods, relapse prevention, and familial support systems are detailed, providing a holistic roadmap. Finally, the book equips readers with an arsenal of Community Resources to aid their transformative journey toward a life free from addiction's grip.

ABOUT THE AUTHOR

Mr. C. P. Kumar is a retired Scientist 'G' from National Institute of Hydrology, Roorkee, Uttarakhand, India. He is also a Reiki Healer and Chakra Balancing practitioner (with pendulum dowsing) and offers Emotional Freedom Technique (EFT) to help individuals with emotional issues. Mr. Kumar has authored many books on technical, spiritual, and social topics.

For further details, you may visit his webpage
https://www.angelfire.com/nh/cpkumar/virgo.html

www.ingramcontent.com/pod-product-compliance
Lightning Source LLC
Chambersburg PA
CBHW071349130726
47996CB00002B/861